Maeve's Poetic Vibes

A Medley of Unusual Poems
and Poetic Thoughts

ELISIENT MAEVE VERNON

WESTBOW
PRESS®
A DIVISION OF THOMAS NELSON
& ZONDERVAN

WestBow Press books may be ordered through booksellers or by contacting:

WestBow Press
A Division of Thomas Nelson & Zondervan
1663 Liberty Drive
Bloomington, IN 47403
www.westbowpress.com
1 (866) 928-1240

Scripture taken from the King James Version of the Bible.

ISBN: 978-1-9736-8050-5 (sc)
ISBN: 978-1-9736-8067-3 (hc)
ISBN: 978-1-9736-8049-9 (e)

Print information available on the last page.

WestBow Press rev. date: 12/26/2019

This book is dedicated to:
My children and grandchildren

I acknowledge the help of my son, Frank, who read the manuscript and gave me valuable suggestions. I also thank him for his contribution to the manuscript along with my other son, Mark.

I thank my husband, Samuel H. Vernon, for the pastoral notes that I copied from the 'Family Table Talk' monthly newsletters that he produced during his tenure as pastor of the Parkway Baptist Church in Miami.

Contents

Introduction xi
Responsibility *by S. H. Vernon* 1

Reflections

Responsibility, Reflection, Realization, Dimension 5
Service: Where do you stand? 6
Overcoming Disappointment *by S. H. Vernon* 7
The Light...8
Forward Look *by S. H. Vernon*..9
Man..10
God Is Out There, Somewhere...11
God's Cure for Loneliness *by S. H. Vernon*......................................13

Tributes

To a Pastor..17
To a Pastor's Wife...19
To Father 20
To a Stepmother: You Gave 22
Tribute to Mom and Dad *by Frank Vernon*..................................... 23
Tribute to a Dear Departed 25
Love: An Important Ingredient *by S. H. Vernon*.............................27

Contemplation

Conviction 31
Eternity Lies Beyond Time..32
The Bridegroom Cometh... 33
The Miracle of Prayer 34
I Grieve for My boy 35
Introspection.. 36
Subconsciousness..37

Nature Played Her Part 38

The Inward Man 41

Letter from a Departed One 42

The Soliloquies of Mary the mother of Jesus 43

Hallelujah! He Is Risen! 47

"He's Alive! He's Alive!" 48

God's Will *by S. H. Vernon* 49

Prayer for the Morning 50

Prayer for the Evening.. 51

Song Lyrics

Lord I Done Wrong... 55

I'll Sing.. 56

There's a Great Revival Brewing 57

I Am on My Way, Lord 58

The Inward, Outward, Upward Man 59

Thank You, O Lord... 60

It's Cool To Be a Christian.. 61

Children's Pages

Growing Up 65

Up and Down 67

Story Time 68

Zacchaeus 69

Your Books 73

Good Citizenship 74

Christmas Recitations 75

The Lord Is King... 76

Prayer 77

Christ's Birthday 78

On the Lighter Side

Eating Is a Pleasure... 81

A Frustrated Dieter.. 82

My Love... 83

Contributing Poets

Daughter: A Father's View *by Frank E. Vernon* 87

Your Graduation *by Frank E. Vernon* 89

The Lord and the Thief *by Mark A. Vernon* 90

When the Bottom Falls Out *by Frank E. Vernon* 92

Christmas Musings *by Frank E. Vernon* 93

About the Author 95

Introduction

If you are reading this introduction, I assume that you have purchased or are thinking of purchasing this book. I have been writing poetry since I was a little girl, writing according to the mood I was in; writing to express an emotion I felt at the time; or writing because I needed a poem for a church program. Some of my poems stayed in my head and never made it to paper. But the book in your hand reflects those that I jotted down in notebooks, scraps of paper, the back of paper napkins or any anything I found at the time.

I am old now and not in good health. My passion is to get my poetry out there for others to enjoy or criticize or be blessed. Putting together this book presented three problems for me:

> First the title – within these covers there is such a mixture of poetry – a kaleidoscope of moods, styles, interests, musings and vibes. I needed an all-inclusive title expressing the whole work;

> Secondly the arrangement – How should I organize the contents. Should it be alphabetical or by theme, length or any old way;

> Thirdly - Should I include prose for a little variety and fillers to fit empty places.

The volume you are holding in your hand is my final decision - my moods confessed -my thoughts expressed.

I hope you, the reader, will read behind the words and find the messages and be blessed.

You will notice – I have added contributions from my husband, S. H. Vernon and my sons, Frank and Mark Vernon. Be blessed!

Responsibility

Some people approach life with the attitude that society owes them a living. The world owes no one a living. Rather, we owe the world a great deal more than we can ever repay. True, we suffer to some extent, as a result of the sins of our fathers, war, crime, unemployment, injustice, etc. But we inherit their blessings too.

The discoveries of science; the world of art and literature; the motor car; gas and electricity; food and clothing, building materials and every blessing of civilization were provided by men and women who realized that they owed the world something.

We should be grateful for the opportunity to live in such a world, a world of such possibilities. The benefits of this world to us are very clear. The burden is upon us to acknowledge with gratitude our indebtedness and take on our responsibilities.

S.H. Vernon

"The heavens declare the glory of God; and the firmament sheweth his handywork."

Psalm 19:1

Reflections

Responsibility, Reflection, Realization, Dimension

REFLECTION
What is it?
It's an ingathering of thoughts. ...
What am I?
Who am I?

REALIZATION
I am a pebble in the vast ocean...
A grain of sand on the shore,
An atom in the mighty universe.
I am only a man.

DIMENSION
It is the love of God for man.
Strength for the weak
Forgiveness for the penitent.
Salvation for the sinner.
Eternal Life!

Service: Where do you stand?

Where do you stand in the arena of things?
Down front in the limelight for all to see
what a wonderful person you've turned out to be?
Or smack in the middle… a great place to hide.
No one will notice you … let your abilities slide…
Where do you stand in the arena of things?
Why not stand humbly in the rear…
willing, available, waiting from God to hear?
How can you serve? How can you share?
The answer is simple… be willing, be there!

Overcoming Disappointment

It is hard to fail and believe that all the dreams we dreamed, the prayers we prayed, the energy we consumed were for nothing. There are words that will console, but perhaps there is also a deeper and what may seem harsher truth that has to be accepted. As Christians we are men and women under obedience, and peace is to be found in the will of God whatever it entails for us.

God's holy will is utterly gracious but not always seen to be kind. God is leading us to glory though sometimes He casts shadows upon our path. Sometimes we may wrestle with Him, argue with Him, and protest, but finally our peace lies in submitting to Him. Such submission will never be easy, but it is not beyond the bounds of possibility that he who accepts it as part of life's discipline will one day do so joyously. The writer to the Hebrews has some wise words to say about the chastening of the Lord. It is a sign of God's love, he says. For a time it may seem painful, but ultimately it yields the fruit of righteousness.

The fruit of disappointment could conceivably be bitterness. It would be a pity if our inflexibility made it so. The glory of God's will is that everything, even a cross, can be a footpath to glory.

S. H. Vernon

The Light

The darkness gathers around me
Suffocating
Choking
Frightening.

I reach out to touch the light beyond
but it is illusive
moving away from the darkness.

The darkness deepens.
I am helpless.
I cry,
"Help me! Save me!"

The Light moves towards me
dispelling the gloom.
"I am The Light."

I bow in penitence and say,
"Show me the way."
I follow The Light.
The darkness is no more.

Forward Look

Before us lies a new year and we are going forth to possess it. Who can tell what we shall find, what new experiences await us, what changes are in store for us?

At the beginning of a new year, we naturally think in both retrospect and prospect. We look on what the past has produced, and think of what the new year may bring, and what dedications and readjustments we ought to make.

As you look back on the past year, you may say sadly, "It's been a hard year what with the threats of terrorists' attack, illness in the family, bereavement and loss, problems and setbacks. Remember in that "backward look" to be thankful for grace to cope with the difficulties. We must not cast a shadow over the new year by seeing only the sad things of the past. We should also recall the sure mercies of God, which are "ever faithful, ever sure", with each new day.

We should not fear what tomorrow may bring, for it is God who holds tomorrow. He is indeed the "Lord who changeth not." Our circumstances may change and our conditions may change, but we love and serve a God who is the same yesterday, today and forever. Let us then be assured that every experience we have had of God's power and blessing in the past ought to increase our faith in His ability to keep us in the future days.

The new year is not only a time to look backward and forward, but to look inward. What does the Lord require of us throughout this year? The true sacrifices of God are a broken spirit, a broken and a contrite heart. If we know this experience, then in this new year we shall really fulfil the word of Micah, which says the real requirement is "to do justly and to love mercy and to walk humbly with Thy God." Micah 6:8

S. H. Vernon

Man

He rises from the dust
The spitting image of the Father.
A cool wind blows.
"Who am I?" his soul cries out to the sky.

"You are a man!"
The voice echoes over the mountains...
The earth stands still for a brief moment,
Then movement begins again—
Rivers meandering through lush green valleys,
Trees sway gently, making soft sounds in the breeze,
Splishing and splashing as fishes rise out of the seas
to view the world then dive beneath the ocean
to live their lives.

Music fills the air as colourful birds slice the atmosphere
in perfect symmetric dance,
singing as they move in perfect rhythm,
glad to be alive, glad to be free in a world
where exists such harmony.

The man stands up.
He stretches his arms upward towards heaven.
His soul reaches out in awe to the Creator.
"I know who I am," he says.
"I am man and You are my Maker.
"You are God.
"I will love You and give You honour and glory always.
For this purpose, was I born."

Note: I think this would, with suitable music, make an inspiring liturgical dance.

God Is Out There, Somewhere

I stand on my balcony and look around.
The mountains and the hills...the horizon smiling in the distance...
The valley alive and flourishing...the sky aglow and beckoning
The whole world, resplendent in its beauty
Tell me that GOD IS OUT THERE, SOMEWHERE.

A gentle wind is blowing. It is the breath of angels.
I look up into the sky and hope to catch a glimpse of an angel.
I see clouds, like cotton candy, floating against a background of clear
blue sky.
The clouds take various shapes and forms
God's angels are making pictures for me.
And I know that GOD IS OUT THERE, SOMEWHERE.

I stare across the big valley of crisp greens
and gaze at the horizon beyond.
I cannot see clearly where the sky ends and the ocean begins,
For the sky seems to dip into the ocean.
But I know GOD IS OUT THERE, SOMEWHERE.

To my left and right are mountains.
Behind me there is a hill.
The mountains, like great big panda bears,
somehow seem protective of the little hill.
But in the evenings when the sun starts its descent.
The great big pandas stretch out their long shadowy arms and
wave a sheet of spooky darkness over the earth.
I am not afraid ... GOD IS OUT THERE, SOMEWHERE.

The mountain on my right stands majestic and tall.
Tiny houses, like little matchboxes, sitting on the mountainside
seem to be nervously awaiting a strong breeze that
would send them toppling down the mountain slopes.
I hold my breath ...I relax.
I know that GOD IS OUT THERE, EVERYWHERE.

God's Cure for Loneliness

S. H. Vernon

"It is not good that man should be alone...." Loneliness is a dreaded and awful enemy. God made two provisions: He surrounded man with the animal creation. What simple joy can come from the company of our pets! Also He instituted marriage, the deepest and most satisfying of all human relationships. "They shall be one flesh".

It is healthy to go back to the beginnings and to glimpse God's intended pattern for the beauty of unity in marriage -- husband and wife sharing their lives together, having a common faith in Jesus Christ as Savior and Lord and sharing a sense of His presence.

It is God's will for the family to enter a covenant of love, respect and mutual concern. In the reverent consciousness of Christ's presence in the home lies the solution to the problem of loneliness.

S. H. Vernon

Tributes

To a Pastor

On this special day, dear pastor,
Your members join the throng
Who come to pay you tribute
In poetry and song.
We join in giving thanks to God
On this your day of days
For He has used you mightily
In many wondrous ways.

We know how you have laboured,
You worked both day and night;
You preached and taught and comforted,
You prayed with all your might;
For you were called to win lost souls,
And strengthen those who're weak;
To encourage those who lost all hope
In Jesus' name to speak.

There have been many times, when
Temptations came your way:
But when you faced such problems
You always stopped to pray.
We know that you have tried so hard
To do God's every will,
And we are proud to see that you
Are being obedient still.

You've passed through bitter waters,
You've had so many foes
And Satan like a monster,
Has thrown so many blows:
But you have fought them skilfully
With Jesus at your side,
With prayer as your weapon and
The Bible as your guide.

You've been a faithful steward,
You've done your work so well,
And many are here, who through you
Will be spared the terrors of Hell.
Now God has brought you safely through
The years of toil and care,
And placed you here in triumph great,
A successful name to bear.

Yes, we are proud, dear Pastor,
And we have come to say,
A big "Thank You" to God
On this significant day;
But there is plenty more to do—
A greater race to run.
So press toward the mark again
And God will say, "Well Done."

To a Pastor's Wife

A lady of talent, a lady of love.
Devout, sincere, a true witness of God's love.
Tactful, gentle, humble and refined --
Sweetness, goodness, and understanding combined.

But she is also made of flesh like you,
With human weaknesses and passions too;
With a woman's need for love and gratitude
And a woman's scorn for the base and crude.

But how often she is misunderstood,
This gentle creature, so kind and good.
Who knows the many tears she's shed
When weary and worn she seeks her bed.

Who knows the anxious thoughts and fears
When sickness in her home appears?
When the bills run high and problems arise,
Who sees the torment in her eyes?

Who knows the lonely hours that come
When her husband is called away from home?
God knows, for very often He hears her pleas
As she seeks for comfort upon her knees.

But oh, my friends, she's not made out of gold,
Give her a sympathetic hand to hold.
A word of comfort and a word of praise
Will help her through her gloomy days.

To Father

Your children celebrate you, Father dear
On this your day of days,
We are glad that we could come today
To join in songs of praise.
We are pleased that we can stand with you
Before this mighty crowd,
For you and our dear mother here
Have made us very proud.

You have lived by Christian principles,
And we shall never forget
What you taught us, not by words alone
But by the examples which you set.
You taught us that a Christian home
Was one where Christ was Head,
Where prayer played a major role
And the Holy Book was read.

You taught us not to compromise
With anything that was wrong,
You taught us that when temptations came
Prayer would make us strong.
We know that you have tried so hard
To do God's every will,
And serving Him these many years
Has been a lifelong thrill.

Your life has not been always smooth,
There have been many blows,
You've had some sad experiences;
Yes, you've had your share of woes.
But you have never succumbed to grief.
Self-pity was not your way,
You fought your problems manfully,
For you always stopped to pray.

Yes, Father, you are leaving prints
Upon the sands of time,
And you will keep on leaving them
Each step of years you climb.
And now we, your children, choose the path
That you these years have trod,
We will follow in your footsteps
And always serve our God.

To a Stepmother: You Gave

You gave of your courage all the years that you spent
In loving and caring for me;
You gave of your courage for few would have bent
To answer the motherless' plea.

You gave of your health, for the work that you did
Required much physical strain,
And often, I guess, you wished you were rid
Of the hardships and mental pain.

You gave of your loyalty, for few would have cared
To risk heartaches and shame;
Disappointments and worries, you must have feared,
And the public abuse of your name.

You gave of yourself as you sacrificed all
Of your time and your labour for me;
For throughout the long years, as I can recall,
You laboured most willingly.

You gave of your service in all phase of life,
To all sorts of folk whom you met;
A more dutiful mother and loving wife,
Has not crossed my path as yet.

And as I reflect on your goodness and love,
On the life you have given away,
I say without doubt, for God is above,
Everyday should be MOTHER'S DAY.

Tribute to Mom and Dad

by Frank Vernon

I thought you would like to know — how much I appreciate the wonderful childhood and upbringing I had as a result of having such wonderful and loving Christian parents in you.

I thought you would like to know — that over the last year my faith has grown by leaps and bounds, and my Christian walk has grown sweeter and sweeter every day.

I thought you would like to know — that I am constantly humbled by the simple truths being revealed to me through the reading of the Word; that it makes me wonder how I did not see them before.

I thought you would like to know — that I now realize that faith grows a step at a time as some small prayer is answered, then another, then another, and so on.

I thought you would like to know — that my family is growing and depending on the Lord more and more each day.

I thought you would like to know — that I know that the scripture verse, *"Train up a child in the way he should go and when he is old, he will not depart from it"* Prov. 22:6, is true.

I thought you would like to know — that I feel as poised as an arrow ready to be let loose as I wait to see what the Lord has in store for me when I graduate.

I thought you would like to know — that whatever prayers you have made to the Lord over me are being answered.

I thought you would like to know — that not only I but my family loves and appreciates you greatly for what you have done for us and the support we can always count on from you.

You are, and have been wonderful parents, parents-in-law, and grandparents. I love you.
I thought you would like to know.

> *(Excerpts from a letter my son wrote us when he was*
> *in college. It was such a blessing to us.)*

Tribute to a Dear Departed

I DO REMEMBER THEE!
I remember, I remember... with great respect to thee,
A mother, a wife, a sister, a friend...
An angel you were to me;
And now you've left this earthly life;
You are from sorrows free.
'Tis with sweet memory of one I loved,
I DO REMEMBER THEE!

I remember, I remember the way you used to smile
When all your children gathered round
To cheer you up awhile.
And when you died, beloved one,
Something died in me;
Now, as I bow my head in prayer,
I DO REMEMBER THEE!

I remember, I remember how hard you worked for me.
You woke each morning with the sun
And laboured willingly.
And when you died, my dearest one,
I cried in agony...
But now with thanks and gratitude
I DO REMEMBER THEE!

I remember, I remember the tears you used to shed
Because of something I had done,
Of something I had said.
And since you left, beloved one
My conscience speaks to me;
And with regret for many things
I DO REMEMBER THEE!

I remember, I remember the sad heart-broken sighs,
And very often 'twas I who caused
The painful, weary cries.
So, if you died with a broken heart,
This is my earnest plea,
That when you reach God's mercy seat,
YOU WILL REMEMBER ME!

Love: An Important Ingredient

Professor Christian Bernard, a pioneer heart transplant surgeon, has been quoted as saying, "We surgeons work inside people, and inside, all people are the same." How true! Whatever the color of our skin or social status, inside we are the same. Snobbery, always a despicable characteristic, is emphatically denounced in the Bible.

We must never judge others by false standards, by what they possess or by their ethnic background; but we must see them as people created by God 'in his own image' and for whom Christ died. Peter, one of the 12 apostles chosen by our Lord, discovered that God has no favorites but that whoever does what is right is acceptable to Him. (Acts 10:34-35).

What Peter discovered is by no means new to the majority of us. Based on that knowledge, some rather commendable attempts have been and are being made to help us to better understand and appreciate each other. We have, however, yet a great way to go! We may have omitted an important ingredient - love. Many of our attempts, commendable as they are, are like bread without leven or cake without sugar. They keep people alive, but they are unappetizing. Similarly, some of our good attempts reflect a charity that has no love.

Jesus befriended everyone with total impartiality. So, we should take courage and with His help and with our own determination strive to emulate Him. "Beloved, let us love one another: for love is of God...." (1 John 4:7).

S. H. Vernon

Unconditional love.

*"I love you when you are good," a father told his small daughter.
The little girl answered quickly, "I love you all the time, Daddy."*

(copied)

Contemplation

Conviction

The Word of God filters through the microphone
reaching into my uttermost being;
Like a two-edged sword it pierces my conscience,
nagging, convicting, persuading.
I must go for cleansing.

But some force pins me to my seat
and I cannot move.
The aisle becomes a widening path
where I must tread to reach the altar.
The pews like steppingstones pan the ever-widening path
putting distance between me and my salvation.

I need only take the first step and
I'd be on my way, but I falter.
I search my mind to find an excuse,
a crutch to lean on, delay tactics,
another path to follow, but it's no use.

There is only one way to Eternal Life.
I take a deep breath. The choice is mine.

Eternity Lies Beyond Time

(Alternate Poem)

I sit in the Sanctuary and the Word of God
filters through the microphone
meandering along the pews until it reaches me.
Its two-edged sword pierces my conscience,
nagging, convicting, persuading.

I know that I must go for cleansing.
Some force fastens me to my seat, and I cannot move.
The aisle becomes like a roaring river
standing between me the Saviour.
In my mind's eye, steppingstones span the river between
my seat and the other shore where lies
the promise of Eternal Life.
I need only take the first step
and I'd be on my way, but I am afraid.

I search my mind to find an excuse,
a crutch to lean on, delay tactics,
another path to follow, but it's no use.
There is only way to the other side.
The decision is mine.
I take a deep breath and I stand.

The Bridegroom Cometh

Light your lamps, the bridegroom cometh.
What? Your lamps are dry?
Hasten to the shops this minute
Ere the bridegroom comes.

Give you some of our oil? Not so!
There is not sufficient to share.
Make haste, off to the shops you go
Ere the bridegroom comes.

Ah, my pretty maids, you are too late
The bridegroom has already come.
He has shut the door. You have missed your date.
The opportunity has gone.

My friend, is your lamp still burning?
Is your lamp still filled with oil?
Be mindful of the soul's great yearning
And be ready when the Bridegroom comes.

Read Matthew 25:1-13

The Miracle of Prayer

I met a downcast, Christian boy
Whose eyes were sad. He had no joy.
I asked him why he did not pray
That Christ would drive the gloom away.
He looked at me and sighed.

How can I see the Saviour's face?
How can I feel His saving grace?
How can I hear the Saviour's voice?
How can it make my heart rejoice?

"By prayer," I replied.

How can I know the Saviour's will?
How can I be obedient still?
How can I know a joy complete?

"By kneeling at the Saviour's feet in prayer," I replied.

Oh, God! I yield myself to Thee.
Send Thou the Holy Ghost on me.
Make me feel that Thou art near
And rid me of this awful fear.
Thus prayerful, he cried.

A happy smile... a look of peace...
And all unhappy thoughts did cease.
His face, a vision of pure joy...
A sigh content... a happy boy
Through the MIRACLE OF PRAYER.

I Grieve for My boy

I grieve for my boy
lost in an unfamiliar world
lost soul in a tiny ship
going round and round
searching for land
in the vast ocean of life.

I grieve for my boy
coming to terms with forbidden feelings
riding on a roller coaster of mixed emotions
bidding each thought one against the other;
feeling the pain of rejection
feeling the agony of guilt
feeling the reality of fear...

I grieve for my boy.
Unable to help with this turmoil in his soul,
I can only continue to pray that one day
he will find true joy and peace
contentment and love, victory o'er sin;
and be a vessel of gold, equipped for service
in God's kingdom on earth.

Introspection

What Could I Have Done Differently?

I look into my soul and ask myself
What could I have done differently?
Could I have taken a different approach when faced with a problem?
Could I have overlooked the little hurts that caused me personal grief
and stretched out my hands in forgiveness and understanding?

What could I have done differently as I prepared my children for life?
Was my discipline too harsh? or too soft?
Was I unfair? Did I not detect each individual need?
Did I set an example of Godly parenting or did I fail in this respect?

What could I have done differently as a wife and mother?
Did I do my best in giving unconditional love?
Or have I been selfish and controlling?
I know I have not been perfect,
But child, I did the best I knew how.
No parent is born with experience.
We gather it along the road of life.
I hope you will forgive me for the mistakes
I made with you as you hope that your children will forgive you
for the mistakes you will make or have made.

After all, if we were perfect, we would not need a Saviour, would we?

Subconsciousness

The place of secrets lies beyond my consciousness,
nagging, convicting, harbouring doubts;
I must go there for inner cleansing that I can move on with my life...

I climb the flight that leads to that place
and wonder what secrets may be lurking there;
With each round of stairs, my limbs grow lighter;
At the top of the stairs, an iron gate swings widely open
and I am propelled to the world beyond;

A clear and gently moving stream obstructs my way.
Beyond the stream lies the answers to my future.
Smooth round steppingstones span the stream
reaching out to grasp the other shore.
But I am afraid.

I look around for another path.
I am mesmerized by the scenery.
What beauty! What splendour!
But the only way to the other side are the steppingstones across the stream.
I take a deep breath.
The future now lies in my hand.

Nature Played Her Part

With weary steps I trudged my way
Upon a lonely hill;
Depression filled my worried soul
And life had lost its thrill.
No one would ever understand
This thing that I would do,
For life held no more promises...
And death was sure and true.

I reached at last the summit high;
I closed my eyes in pain.
This day would end my troubled soul...
I'd never grieve again.
With trembling hands...I brought it forth...
This weapon, gleaming bright...
And as I put it to my ear
I closed my eyes so tight.

But ere I made the final move
To end my life of woe,
I'd take my last and longest look
At the scenery just below.
With weary sigh I opened my eyes
And there beheld the view...
A wondrous...marvellous...sight it was!
So old, yet ever new!

The sea was like a crystal glass
Of slightly varied hue;
And as a background to the clouds
The sky was clearest blue.
The little yachts within the bay
All played a striking part
In this last hour...this precious hour...
Ere stilled my beating heart.

The mountains on my right did stand
In elegance and pride;
And the coral rocks within the cove
Could not their beauty hide.
The graceful lilies in the breeze
Seemed to beckon me
Inviting me to see that life
Was not all misery.

But oh! the sight that caught my eyes
And calmed my inward fears
Was the symbol of God's promise true...
It wiped away my tears;
For there, beyond the ocean wide,
Behind the mountains high...
Was a picture...a painting in perfect blend...
A rainbow in the sky!

Yes, nature was awake and real!
But I was doomed to die
Because my grief had blinded me.
Satan had been sly.
I thrust the weapon from my hand
And fell upon my knee...
I prayed for strength to conquer grief
That I, at last might see.

With newfound strength, I found my way
Down that lonely hill.
Courage filled my happy soul...
There was a new-born will.
No one else might understand
This change within my heart,
How through her wondrous splendour
NATURE HAD PLAYED HER PART!

The Inward Man

The outward man is perishing,
As the years take their toll and we waste away
But the inward man is quickening
With our soul's renewal each day.

The inward man grows stronger
As we bear the stress, enduring the pain
For we look towards the morrow
When with Jesus we shall reign.

The upward man is strengthening
For by faith we see the end of the road
Endurance rewarded, and achieving
Heaven as our final abode.

So, never give up, dear Christian
Though your troubles are stressful and hard
The future is bright and promising
With eternity's final reward.

~~~~~~~~~~~~~~~~

I don't feel the pressure
Of a load of sin,
For God has forgiven me;
I have peace within.

Letter from a Departed One

Dear Loved Ones:

I've been at the edge of the river for so long.
The suffering has been intense ...
But now, I have passed over.
What relief!

My Saviour was waiting for me with open arms
As I knew He would.
Living for Christ has paid off.
My home with the Father is more than human tongue can describe.
How foolish are those who reject His Son, Jesus!

I can see your tears ... your loneliness ... your grief.
But mourning is just for a while.
Get ready to meet me when you, too, shall have passed beyond the river.
I will be waiting here, with my Saviour.

The Soliloquies of Mary the mother of Jesus

AT THE CROSS

O, Cross! Wretched cross! Thou cruel tree!
Thou instrument of agony!
O, had I but the strength to tear thy cruel limbs apart,
I'd cast thy shattered fragments where no one could find a part.
How didst thou feel thou wooden one
as thou didst bare my noble Son?
As thou didst witness the cruel deed
which caused the Holy One to bleed?

Didst thou feel honoured that thy wooden frame,
Though it held the body, withheld the blame?
I doubt that thou canst feel, O Cross,
but I resent my bitter loss.
And yet, unfeeling cross, I envy thee
for thou canst feel no agony;
Thou hast no human heart within;
Thou hast no consciousness of sin;
But thou art still a sign to me
of this world's scorn and cruelty.

AT THE TOMB

O, Jesus, my Son, asleep in the tomb,
the best of all sons conceived in a womb,
Cans't Thou not hear Thy mother's heart-broken cry
as she kneels by the rock where Thou dost lie?

As a Babe I watched Thee with tenderest care.
Thou wast always so loving, so willing to share;
But I always recalled the High Priest's word
that one day my heart would be pierced with a sword.
As the years sped by, I saw Thy fate,
for Thou wast a target of spite and hate.

The enemies of goodness were always conniving
against a work that in power was striving...
'till at last they took Thee, my Master, my Son!
Thou wast MOCKED...and SCORNED...and SPAT UPON.
Thou wast beaten with whips and crowned with thorns
and THRUST in a grave, ere another day dawns.

I loved Thee, Lord Jesus, my Master and Son...
But Thou wast only a loan from the Heavenly One;
And now, Thou art gone, I should not weep
for Thou art not dead; Thou art only asleep.
But still, I AM human. I cannot control
the tears of sorrow that down my cheek roll. *(pause)*

The night is far spent, and all is at rest;
But I am not happy. I'm sorely distressed...
Indeed, Thou didst warn us that one day You'd be
snatched from our presence and nailed to a tree,
thrown in a grave and buried in sin....
But that there would the work of Salvation begin.
I listened, My Son, but could not comprehend.
Didst Thou mean that this will not be the end?

Thou wast good in every thought and deed.
Forgiveness and love was ever Thy creed.
Even as Thou didst hang in pain,
there was no bitterness, no sad complain.
"Forgive them, Father," Thou didst cry.
Forgive the one's who'd made Thee die—?
Nay, Son. I fail to understand
how Thou couldst do a thing so grand.

AT THE TOMB AFTER THE RESURRECTION

Jesus is risen? I scarce can believe!
No more need I sorrow? No more need I grieve?
I buried a Son...but a Saviour arose
from Whom love and forgiveness and sympathy flows.
Oh, faithless sinner that I wast,
So filled with doubts, so lacking in trust,
Was there ever a moment so happy ...so sweet...
so free from sorrows...so sure, so complete!
Oh, Jesus, my Saviour, my heart overflows.
I love Thee, I love Thee, as nobody knows.
Thou art no more my son, but my Saviour! My God!
And I am a sinner, redeemed by Thy blood.

At the Cross

O Cross that's now aglow with light,
where love hath won the bitter fight,
I look on thee with new respect
for now, I clearly can detect
that thou wast chosen—a symbol of love!
An expression from God, our Father above.

I once was walking in the darkness of sin,
But thou wast the way that let the Light in;
And through the great work that thou didst do
in bearing the Saviour, the Lamb of God who
gave His dear life an atonement for sin,
the work of Redemption did at once begin.

And now I do cherish Thee, thou cross of Light.
And all who do likewise with God will unite.
I see thee no more as a cross of gloom
condemning an innocent One to the tomb,
But now I do see thee, Love's fires ablaze!
A symbol of purity! A symbol of praise!
And now with great joy, Hallelujah, I'll sing
Hallelujah to Jesus! My Saviour! My King!

~~~~~~~~~~~~~~~~

Hallelujah! He Is Risen!

The tomb is empty. The grave lay bare.
Jesus, the crucified is no longer there.
"He is risen," the angel said.
"Go, tell His disciples He's no longer dead."
"He is risen! He is risen!"

With urgent steps we too must go
To shout it and tell it,
and let the whole world know,
"Jesus is risen! And we must sing
hallelujahs to Him, our Saviour and King."
"Hallelujah! Hallelujah!"

"He's Alive! He's Alive!"

Do not cry. Do not mourn.
Let your grief come to an end
Do not sigh, look forlorn.
Your broken heart will mend
when you hear the good news...
"He's alive! He's alive!"

God's Will

To some people God's will is medicine - a pill to get rid of life's ills. To others, God's will is something to be borne. - when adversity comes, we must bear it. To yet others, it is the sweet at the end of a meal - it gives taste to life. But to Jesus it was basic - neither medicine, nor a burden nor a sweet, but a meal.

As the body is made for food so the spirit is made for the will of God. Self-will is self-poison; God's will is self-fulfillment. There is no healthier person than the one in line with God's will, for this supplies the right spiritual vitamins to revitalize him. We need to pray for liberty from ourselves in order that our meat and drink will be that of doing the will of God!

by S. H. Vernon

Prayer for the Morning

Heavenly Father, thank You for the night's rest. You provided me with a roof over my head and safety through the night. And now You have brought me to the beginning of a new day.

Beginnings give me a fresh start, so I ask You to renew my heart with Your strength and purpose. Forgive me the sins and mistakes I made yesterday and help me not to make the same mistakes today.

Provide for me this day all the necessities of life and help me to be ever grateful for all that I receive from You. Shine through me so that everyone I meet today may feel Your presence in my life. Let me be a blessing to others. Take my hand, precious Lord, and lead me through this day. It is in Jesus' name I pray, Amen.

Prayer for the Evening

Lord, it is evening hours and I come to You weary in body but feeling joyful in my soul. I sit on my porch and look around and ask myself, "Where is that wind coming from? Who controls the setting sun? It is gorgeous in the western sky, golden and yellow streaks forming patterns behind the clouds. Little birds are hurrying to their place of rest."

I know, O God, that You are out there somewhere.

I feel so small in this great universe. You are such an awesome God, our great Creator, and I am undeserving of Your mercy and love. But I do feel comforted that You are concerned for my wellbeing. So Heavenly Father, I ask You to forgive my sins of today, and let Your Holy Spirit continue to convict me whenever I stray from the righteous path. I will rest in peace tonight for You will be with me.

I pray also for my family, my church family and all those in need all over the world. Let Your Holy Spirit convict the unsaved that they may come to accept Your Son, the Lord Jesus Christ, and it is in His name I pray, Amen.

Song Lyrics

(NOTE: I am praying that some inspired musician will take these lyrics and put them to music.)

Lord I Done Wrong

Lord I done wrong.... and I feel so sad,
Please forgive me .... and make me glad.
I am sorry Lord.... that I betrayed You.
Please tell me what .... I ought to do,
For I done wrong and I feeling bad.

Lord I done wrong.... I broke Your heart;
I betrayed You, Jesus.... right from the start.
I'm a worthless coward .... and foolish too.
Please tell me what .... I ought to do,
For I done wrong when I broke Your heart,

Lord I done wrong .... I caused You grief;
My soul is hurting .... and I need relief.
Please forgive me .... for being so weak;
Peace of mind .... is what I seek,
For I done wrong when I caused You grief

Lord I done wrong .... please hear my prayer.
My guilt is heavy .... too much to bear;
I need forgiveness .... Take away my sin.
Wash me now, Lord .... make me clean again.
Lord I done wrong. Please hear my prayer.

Thank You, Jesus! ... You have set me free!
You took my burdens ... at Calvary...
The weight is gone,... and now I'm whole.
Thank You, Jesus, ... You've saved my soul.
Thank You, Jesus, ... at last I'm free!

I'll Sing

When I sing about my Saviour
His Spirit fills my soul
When I sing about my Jesus
His Presence makes me whole.

So, I'll sing.
I'll lift my voice to heaven, and I'll sing.
I will talk to my Redeemer and I'll sing.
I will worship Him forever and I'll sing, sing, sing
To my King.

When I sing about His love
I feel a changing mood.
When I sing about His sacrifice
I am filled with gratitude

So, I'll sing.
I'll lift my voice to heaven and I'll sing.
I will talk to my Redeemer and I'll sing.
I will worship Him forever and I'll sing, sing, sing
To my King.

I will sing away my tears
When I'm feeling low in spirit
And my mind is filled with gloom
And tears are in my eyes.

Yes, I'll sing.
I'll lift my voice to heaven, and I'll sing.
I will talk to my Redeemer and I'll sing.
I will worship Him forever, and I'll sing, sing, sing
To my King.

There's a Great Revival Brewing

There's a great revival brewing
And I want to be a part,
Lord, break my stubborn spirit
And give me a Christ-like heart.

There's a great revival brewing
And I want to be a part,
Lord, as I keep on praying
Let revival in me start.

There's a great revival brewing
And I want to be a part,
Lord, give me strength and boldness
Your message to impart.

There's a great revival brewing
O Spirit treat my soul!
Prepare me, cleanse me, teach me
To reach the Savior's goal.

I Am on My Way, Lord

I am on my way, Lord, I am on my way,
To face again another day.
I read Your Word, convicting, healing,
Strengthening and cleansing, compelling, revealing.
Yes, Lord, I am on my way, I am on my way,
To face again another day.

I am on my way, Lord, I am on my way,
To face again another day.
I fall on my knees and I seek Your guidance,
I need Your protection, and crave Your endurance;
Yes, Lord, I am on my way, I am on my way,
To face again another day.

I am on my way, Lord, I am on my way,
To face again another day.
I give You my will Lord, and my stubborn pride
I seek Your forgiveness; please stay by my side
As I go on my way, Lord, as I go on my way,
To face again another day.

The Inward, Outward, Upward Man

The outward man is perishing, (perishing, perishing)
The outward man is perishing
As our bodies waste away.
But the inward man is quickening, (quickening, quickening)
The inward man is quickening,
When our soul is renewed each day.

The inward man grows stronger, (stronger, stronger)
The inward man grows stronger,
Enduring stress and pain.
For we look towards tomorrow, (tomorrow, tomorrow,)
We look towards tomorrow
When with Jesus we shall reign.

The upward man is strengthening, (strengthening, strengthening)
The upward man is strengthening,
Through faith and trust in God.
The future is bright and promising, (promising, promising)
The future is bright and promising,
With eternity's final reward.

So, never give up, dear Christian, (dear Christian, dear Christian)
So never give up, dear Christian,
For Heaven is the final abode.
For those who receive Salvation, (Salvation, Salvation)
Yes those who receive Salvation
Will come to the end of the road.

Based on 2 Corinthians 4:16

Thank You, O Lord

Thank You, O Lord for the sunshine
Thank You, O Lord for the rain
Thank You, O Lord for the moonlight
Thank You, again and again.

Thank You, O Lord for the splendor
Of nature awake in the Spring
The tall trees that look up in wonder
The manifold birdies that sing.

Thank You, O Lord for protection
Thank You, O Lord for our food
Thank You, O Lord for provision
And all You provide for our good.

Remembering You're the Creator
The One who rules over all
There is no one who is greater
So thank You for everything great or small.

It's Cool To Be a Christian

It's cool, it's cool, it's cool to be a Christian!
It's cool, it's cool, it's cool to praise the Lord.
It's cool, it's cool, it's cool to talk to Jesus!
It's cool, it's cool, it's cool to read God's Word.

It's cool, it's cool, it's cool to follow Jesus!
It's cool, it's cool, it's cool to see the Light.
It's cool, it's cool, it's cool to stand up bravely!
It's cool, it's cool, it's cool to do what's right.

It's cool, it's cool, it's cool to tell my peer group!
It's cool, it's cool, it's cool, the choice I've made.
It's cool, it's cool, it's cool to live for Jesus!
It's cool, it's cool, it's cool to serve the Lord.

Children's Pages

(NOTE: Some poems were written as recitations for little children to say in a Christmas program.)

Growing Up

When I was born, I could not stand
I could not walk, nor wave my hand
I could not talk… I could not sit
I was too small to do a thing
But then, I soon began to grow;
I learned to smile and hold my toe.
My eyes grew round, and very big
And I was FAT… as Pigling Pig.

I kept on growing, and learning too
Many tricks and games, like "Peek-a-boo".
When I could run around and play,
I kept Mom busy every day.
I learned to dress and feed myself;
I was a happy little elf.
Every day I grew and grew,
And before you knew it, I was TWO.

Then I was THREE, then I was FOUR,
And still I kept on growing more.
"You're getting big," said everyone.
Soon Dad will have a great big son.
Then I was FIVE, and now I'm SIX,
And I've put aside all baby tricks.
I now can COUNT and READ and WRITE;
My teacher says, I'm very bright.

Now, Daddy has just promised me
That I may join the LIBRARY:
For I can write my name real well,
And I can read, and I can spell.
"Books can help your mind to grow,"
It's true, for my daddy told me so.
I'll keep on growing in every way,
So, watch out! I will be BIG someday.

Up and Down

When I stand on my feet
I am right side UP.
My feet are DOWN
And my head is UP.
When I stand on my feet
I am right side UP.

When I stand on my head
I am upside DOWN.
My feet are UP
And my head is DOWN.
When I stand on my head
I am upside DOWN.

When I do a somersault
I am UP and DOWN.
My feet are UP
When my head is DOWN.
Then my head goes UP
And my feet come down.

So UP and DOWN
or DOWN and UP
A safe place to be is
To stand on my feet.
So my head is UP
And. my feet are DOWN.

"I will praise You, for I am fearfully and wonderfully made."
Psalm 139:14

Story Time

A sea of curious eyes stare at me
Waiting...
Expecting something.
A promise?
A seed of knowledge?
Entertainment?

I stare at the innocent faces and panic.
It's a heavy responsibility!
Can I reach into their souls?
Give hope?
Light a spark?
Motivate?

Someone smiles. I smile. All smile.
The moment of tension is over.
I begin. "Once upon a time..."
Little chests rise and fall.
Bated breath!
... Happily, ever after.

Zacchaeus

Zacchaeus was a clever crook
as we have read in the Holy Book.
His riches grew as he robbed the poor,
and still in his greed he wanted more.
In physical form, he was not tall.
The Bible says he was very small.
It seems that he was curious too
for what the Bible says is true.

We're told that he had greatly desired
to see the Man whom the people admired;
This Jesus of Nazareth is the Saviour, they claimed,
Who had cured the blind, the dumb and the lamed.
Yes, Zacchaeus was curious, and perhaps too
the Spirit of God had a work to do
in the life of this man, so sinful and bad,
who had made many people so despairingly sad.

Then, one day it was rumoured about
that Jesus was coming, and Zacchaeus no doubt
Felt that this was an opportune time to inspect
the Man who'd demanded such holy respect.
But Zacchaeus knew that he'd never see
the Saviour unless he climbed a tree;
For the crowd was so large, it would form a wall
which would block the vision of a man so small.

And so, we see Zacchaeus bending his knee
as he climbed up into the Sycamore tree;
He made himself comfy, since he had to wait
for this famous Personality to pass his gate.
He kept his eyes on the dusty road,
and the tension he built up, nearly made him explode;
Then at last, he heard a faint sound...
His heart missed a beat, then began to pound.

A cyclone of dust in the distance arose
and Zacchaeus was trembling from his head to his toes.
So deep were his feelings, he could scarcely control
the powerful yearning in his sin-sick soul.
As the dust came nearer and nearer and nearer
He could now see the great crowd, for his vision was clearer.
His excitement being multiplied, he almost arose
but remembered in time his precarious pose.

The Master was coming! At last he would see
This popular Carpenter of Galilee.
"Is He really the Christ as the people proclaim?"
Does He honestly bear Jehovah's name?"
Trot-trot! Clop-clop! ...the sounds grew loud,
As on came the Carpenter, the donkeys, the crowd.
And Zacchaeus was in an emotional glee
As he looked down from out of the Sycamore tree

All of a sudden, the great crowd stopped!
Zacchaeus was so surprised, he almost dropped!
Oh! Who is that looking up in the tree?
The Master? The Saviour? Could it really be?
All was silent. The earth stood still.
And who can describe the publican's thrill
When all of a sudden, the silence broke
And the calm, sweet voice of the Saviour spoke?

"Zacchaeus, Zacchaeus, descend that tree.
This day I must abide with thee."
Zacchaeus scarce could comprehend;
Did Jesus mean to be his friend?
"Oh Lord and Master!" was his cry,
"Do You mean, to abide with such as I?"
And there arose a protest great
From those who stood without the gate.

"Does the Master really mean to dine
With this thief? this filthy swine?"
But Zacchaeus cared not what they said,
Down from the Sycamore tree he sped.
And though his heart was stained with sin,
He joyfully welcomed the Saviour in.

And with repentant heart he cried,
"Oh Lord, my sins I'll put aside."
"I will sell my goods and give to the poor,
The innocent folk, I'll rob no more.
And to those whom I have caused much pain,
I'll restore fourfold to them again.

When Zacchaeus thus, himself had bared,
The people around just stood and stared.
"Is it possible"' they cried, "that this well-known thief
Has come to accept the Christian belief?'
The Saviour stilled them with a look -
And when He spoke, the whole earth shook.

"This day is salvation come to thee,
For I came to set the sinner free."
The heavens opened - joy bells rang
The saints did smile - angels sang
There was rejoicing on earth and in heaven,
For Zacchaeus had had his sins forgiven."

Based on Luke 19:1-9

 Your Books

You must learn to care your books,
Help preserve their nice clean looks.
Hold them gently, and with care
Turn their pages lest they tear.

They're not children to be fed
With fruits and sweets and buttered bread;
They are not for your dirty hands,
Nor bits of pencils, nor rubber bands.

So, take great care of all your books,
And preserve their nice clean looks.

Good Citizenship

There are many ways that you can help
To build a better Isle;
You can do it by your courtesy,
By your winning, pleasant smile.

'Tis not enough to say that you
Are much too young or small;
For there are many, many things
That can be done by all.

There are lots of little things that count;
And some I'll mention here;
Be honest, clean, upright and kind
And you'll have done your share.

Christmas Recitations

WHAT CAN I GIVE TO JESUS?

What can I give to Jesus who came to sinful earth?
Who though a Holy Infant was born of humble birth?
What can I give to Jesus who was a child like me?
Who loved to laugh and sing and play so merrily?

What can I give to Jesus who grew to be a Man?
Who worked so many miracles according to God's plan?
What can I give to Jesus who died for sinful me?
Who rose again in glory to set the sinner free?

What can I give to Jesus?
I give myself today.
My heart I'll give, Lord Jesus, oh make me Thine I pray.

MY GIFTS

I'll give my mother a gift today
And say, "Merry Christmas to you.";
I'll give Lord Jesus my heart today
And say, "Happy Birthday to You!"

The Lord Is King

The Lord Is King and we have come to worship Him
So, clap your little hands – clap, clap, clap, clap,
and stamp your little feet – thump, thump, thump, thump.
And sing a song of praise to Him.

The Lord Is King and we have come to worship Him
So beat your little drums – boom, boom, boom, boom;
And play your little flutes – ooh, ooh, ooh, ooh.
And sing a song of praise to Him

The Lord Is King and we have come to worship Him
So, bend your little knees- and kneel in prayer
and clasp your little hands - and close your eyes
As you say a prayer of thanks to Him.

Prayer

I pray to You, Lord Jesus, on this blessed Christmas Day.
Be with me every moment and guide me in every way.
Let Your will be my will in the choices that I make.
I'm leaning on your promises, so I won't make a mistake

When burdens bear me down, please carry them for me.
Help me not to feel discouraged, I look for help from Thee.
In my daily chores I'll honour You with gratitude and love
I'll call upon You, Lord Jesus, Precious Saviour from above

Bless all my friends and family and keep them in Your care
And to those who do not know Thee, the gospel I must share.
For my sinful soul, Lord Jesus, that Satan has defiled
Dear Lord, forgive me, forgive Your erring child.

Amen

Christ's Birthday

It's Christ's birthday, I'm sure you know;
But what have I to give to One who gave Himself for me
That I might look and live?

I cannot give Him any gold,
For He has more than I;
He owns the earth with all its wealth, the ocean and the sky.

But I can give myself to Him;
My feet to walk His ways;
My little hands to do His will; my lips to sing His praise.

And I can give a smile to all
Who pass me every day;
And I can find for those who're sad, a kindly word to say.

I'll try my best to please my Lord
In action, word and deed;
And doing good to all I meet will be my daily creed.

On the Lighter Side

Eating Is a Pleasure

Eating is a pleasure.
I'm sure you think so, too;
Though often it may have effects
Upon the size of you.
But if you don't mind being fat
I sure will recommend
That you just eat and sleep and chat
And nature will amend.

Eating is a pleasure;
But as the years go by
And you see yourself as others do
I'm sure you'll feel to cry.
Your waist has doubled in its size
Your hips, there is not measure.
So, if you want a good advice
Don't eat too much for pleasure.

A Frustrated Dieter

I've made up my mind to be fat.
Now what do you think of that?
There's too much at stake
Like donuts and cake
And chicken wings fried up in fat.

When the smells drive me wild
I'm just like a child
Not knowing at which point to stop;
So, I cheat, and I eat,
I indulge and I bulge
And gorge till I'm ready to pop.

When the craving has passed
I pray and I fast
I'm determined to try once again.
As I deal with my guilt,
My strength is rebuilt
And confidence I once more regain.

My Love

You are my delight
Angel of morn and night;
Thy tender lips of honeyed dew
Shall upon my lips bestrew
The essence of thy love.

You are my desire;
Fill me with love's great fire;
Give me thy hands to cool my brow
Thy rosy cheeks to soothe me now
For I am consumed with love.

Contributing Poets

My sons:
Frank E. Vernon
Mark A. Vernon

Daughter: A Father's View

by *Frank E. Vernon*

You are beautiful to behold,
The texture of your skin,
The shape of your eyes,
A mesmerizing glimmer of your mom
With a hint of your dad.
Yet your outward beauty is nothing
To that which shines from within

I see a light of genuine warmth
That spreads to all around,
A soul that overflows with love
For those who need your help,
A smile that's beautiful and infectious
And a mind that's full of great ideals

The Lord has truly blessed me
With a daughter of amazing talent
Lord, I truly love her
And on my knees to You I pray
Please show her how to channel
These awesome gifts from You
To demonstrate Your love
And glorify Your name

Oh dear daughter, I love you so,
Forgive a foolish father
Who sees your faults, yet is blind
To the beautiful person created by God
Your fathers love you.
One knows you're special and
One created you for a special purpose
That only you can fulfill

So, this is my prayer, dear daughter
That you will find that special purpose
And know true joy that the Father gives
To those who live within His will
A peace that passes all understanding
And unimaginable rewards laid up in heaven
That cannot be destroyed.

Your Graduation

by Frank E. Vernon

The time has finally come
You have overcome the tests,
The challenging times,
the obstacles that came and went
You took everything in stride.

Now you must face the world
The true test of your training.
I have no doubt that you'll overcome
The secret is Christ at the centre
"In all your ways acknowledge Him
And He will direct your path."

Don't take your family for granted
They helped you get here
Because they supported you.
They provided a net that caught you
When bad days tried to bring you down.
They love you unconditionally

I am proud of you, my friend
My heart is overjoyed
if ever you need a listening ear
Remember me. I will not judge
But seek God's wisdom to impart.
Congratulations! You are a Champion!

The Lord and the Thief

by Mark A. Vernon

Never have I felt such pain as on this day
I hang from a cross having lost my way
Who are you oh man to claim right now
Your righteous kingdom to which we bow?
I see no angels or lightning strike
To protect a God from human strife
Be gone with you, oh King of Jews
Hell awaits both me and you

Look at you all battered and braised
Saviour you say to both Gentile and Jew
Climb down from that cross oh Son of God
Strike us with your mighty rod
What God would bear such degrading blows
When he could easily destroy his foes
Your face is lined with pain as mine
No King on earth would he so kind

I am a sinner and so are you
Why not face it? You're just a Jew
Your forehead bleeds with your hands and feet
What God would love and bear such heat
Why do you lie there so meek and mild?
We've scoffed and spat and called you vile
Yet you say and do things most surprising
Caring for others while you poise dying

"Father forgive us?" did I hear you right
What manner of man would care in your plight?
Truly you are the Most Holy Son of God
Sent to redeem us on this earthly sod
My Christ! My King! Most Precious One!
Would you forgive God's wayward son?
The time is near, death waves its wand
With you my Lord, the battle's won

"Remember me, Jesus, as you claim your Kingdom"
My time of judgment doth rapidly come
What joy, what peace, your love entice
With words, "Today, you'll join me in Paradise!"
Saved from damnation, not a moment to spare
My Lord and my King, I'm thankful You're here.

When the Bottom Falls Out

by Frank E Vernon

I went to work one day.
To my surprise I was called to see my boss.
Without much ado, he told me I had no job.
My heart skipped a beat.
I struggled to process the news.
I could not believe my ears.
My stomach was in a whirl.
I fought to keep a poker face.
I would not show my hurt.

I was utterly devastated. I could not let him see.
Was this it then? Was I a failure?
What would I tell my family?
Is this why people take their lives?
How could this happen to me?
Then from within I heard a still soft voice.
"This job does not define you.
It does not control your fate. I do."

Upon my knees I fell and said:
"Yes, Lord You do. In Your hands, I leave it."
A peace fell upon me.
In my Savior's grace I rested.
I snuggled close in my Savior's arms.
Contentment closed around me.

Christmas Musings

by Frank F. Vernon

People rushing to and fro
excitement in the air
Lights are flashing
and children chattering
Christmas time is here!

I hear the radio booming as Christmas carols play
There are decorations everywhere.
What a joyous day.
Christmas trees are bright and glittering,
yards are all aglow.
Stores are full of shoppers searching
for the perfect gift to go.

Here in my cocoon of silence I look out and I wonder.
Do they know the reason for the season?
Do they know that my Saviour born
thousands of years ago was the greatest Gift ever given?
Do they know He came and died that they might live?
Do they know the God of the universe would like to be their friend?
Do they not realize the season is just a blip in light of eternity?

Lord, I pray that in this season amidst all the hustle and bustle
People will hear Your Spirit full of grief at being forgotten
and in a moment of clarity and remorse get on their knees
and give You thanks and praise in awe and wonder
for the greatest Gift ever given.

Lord, make it a Christmas to remember
as people of every race and gender
will come to know the greatest love of all.
A love that knows no bounds, perfect and unconditional;
A love that will last throughout eternity
providing joy beyond compare.

About the Author

Elisient Maeve Vernon spent most of her life in children's ministry. She worked with children in the churches pastored by her husband Rev. Samuel Vernon who is now retired from full time ministry.

Mrs. Vernon spent her early years in a rural village in Jamaica where her father was the pastor. She was a tomboy, the only girl among several brothers. After High School she was trained as a children's librarian. She worked in the Library Services in Jamaica, Trinidad and Western Canada.

Mrs. Vernon's studies in child psychology, writing for children and the Bible were evidences that God had prepared her to become a children's editor for Caribbean Christian Publications (CCP). She served 11 years as editor of "Caribbean Bible Lessons" for younger children (7-9 years).

Since retirement she has busied herself in preparing some of her many manuscripts for publication. She has published to date three children's books and two books of Christian plays, listed below: *Ava's Bad Day, More Ava Stories,* (ages 2-5) *Coconut Fun* (ages 9-12) and *Christmas Miracles: A Baby in the Manger and other plays,* are all available on Amazon. *The Truth of the Resurrection: He Is Risen, and other plays* was published by Fairway Press in 1995 and is not available at the moment.

Mrs. Vernon now resides with her husband of 65 years in Miami, Florida.

Printed in the United States
By Bookmasters